How to Get Promoted

Simple Steps to Better Title and Higher Pay

How to Get Promoted

Simple Steps to Better Title and Higher Pay

By Anthony S. Park

Dedication

For my wife and corporate guru, Hanna

Thank you for your feedback

Hearing directly from you, the reader, is the best way for me to make these books as useful as possible.

Please share how this book has helped you, or any suggestions for how I can make it better. You can email me at promoted@anthonyspark.com or text me at 212-401-2990.

I thank you in advance for your feedback.

Best,
Anthony

TABLE OF CONTENTS

INTRODUCTION

Why do some folks die richer than others?

As a professional executor (someone who helps settle the estate of a person who has died), I've seen hundreds of final net worths. More importantly, I've seen which financial choices and habits seem to be linked to higher net worth— things such as owning your own business and compound investing (both of which I'll write about in other books).

But the financial game-changer that's the most accessible to the most people? Maximizing your career earnings from your 9-5 job.

You've probably heard some of the latest trends for making more money: start a side hustle. Buy Bitcoin. Become an influencer (selfie!). But the easiest "life hack" – the money that's just sitting on the table, waiting for you to pick it up— is to get promoted at work, and to get paid what you deserve.

And it seems like we all know it. 40% of U.S. employees believe they are underpaid, and 75% of Gen Z workers believe they should be promoted in their first year.

So what's the problem? Well, too many of us fumble about when asking for a promotion. Or worse yet, we never ask at all.

And it's easy to understand why: we spend time improving our skills and trying to do our best at our jobs. But very few of us receive any counseling, mentoring, or education on how to manage our own *career advancement.*

WHO IS THIS BOOK FOR?

I wrote this book for the Dilberts of the world. The folks who live in the *Office Space* universe. Basically, anyone working in corporate America.

If you're a professional (e.g., a lawyer, accountant, etc.) or work in a specialized industry (e.g., finance, venture capital, etc.), this book is still for you. Most of the general principles can apply to your situation.

Alas, this book is not so much for people in professions with rigid, tenure-based hierarchies, such as government, military, or union-backed jobs. Those occupations often have unique rules and career paths. But again, much of the guidance here will still be helpful.

Lastly, I've written this book for any stage of your career: from entry-level all the way up to senior management. So even if you are well into your career and think you've been moving up nicely, let's see if we can do even better.

THE GOAL OF THIS BOOK

If I could leave you with just three takeaways, they'd be:

1. Getting consistently promoted is not about asking a one-off question: it's a *campaign* of months, even years.

2. It's all about *communication*—from broadcasting your accomplishments (someone has to toot your horn) to making sure your boss knows you want a promotion (he can't read your mind).

3. You must *think long-term.* Getting proper promotions is not just about the immediate satisfaction of a pat on the back, new title, and more money. These are all great, no doubt. But it's also about making sure your resume is rock solid and you don't let your boss or company start inadvertently taking you for granted. That's a slippery slope.

A BRIEF OUTLINE

In Chapters 1 through 3, I'll cover the basics, including what a "promotion" means, getting a raise without a promotion, and why consistent promotions are so important for your career.

In Chapters 4 through 7, I'll detail the step-by-step checklist of things you must do *before* you even think of asking for a promotion: excel at your current job, show you're ready for more, get noticed, and make sure your boss know you're gunning for that promotion.

In Chapter 8, you'll learn about timing, such as how often you should seek promotions, and how to read the terrain before asking.

Chapters 9 and 10 are all about the ask: how to prepare for and manage your actual conversation with your boss.

Lastly, in Chapter 11, I'll talk about what happens after the conversation: following up (remember, it's a campaign) and what to do if you do (or don't) get the promotion.

Let's get started.

CHAPTER 1.

WHAT A PROMOTION MEANS FOR YOUR CAREER

Imagine your boss comes to your cube to tell you he has some "great news" about your job. You probably feel excited, but maybe uncertain about what to expect—especially if this is the first time it's happening. The news may be unclear and leave you to wonder, "Did I actually get promoted?" or "What exactly *is* a promotion?"

Most of us probably think of promotions as a reward for high performance, but they happen for a variety of reasons. Often, there's a vacancy due to another employee leaving, or company growth that requires someone else to move up. Or, management might promote an employee out of fear that he or she will leave the company. People can even receive promotions out of necessity, such as when a novice worker needs to quickly fill the shoes of someone who unexpectedly retires.

MAJOR CHANGES TO EXPECT

No matter the circumstances, a promotion is about more than getting a pat on the back and a higher salary for your hard work. In this section, you'll learn how to recognize the changes that come along with getting promoted.

New title and more pay

Many (although not all) promotions come with a more senior title and an increase in pay. Most professionals look forward to a title change because it feels great to be recognized at work. It gives you a feeling of prestige and progress; it shows your coworkers that you're moving up in the organization; and it demonstrates your growth to future employers and recruiters.

For example, imagine a hiring manager or recruiter from another company is seeking a new candidate—someone with a background and skillset similar to yours. Recruiters and managers are typically scanning dozens, if not hundreds, of resumes to discover the right candidate. They don't necessarily look at each resume or Linkedin profile in depth—they simply don't have the time.

However, a recruiter *will* look at your career timeline to assess your progression. If it looks like you've been in the same position for three or four years, it can appear that you're stagnant or complacent in your career.

On the flip side, imagine the recruiter sees that you've been promoted twice at your current company in the last three and a half years. You started out as a junior analyst, were promoted to an analyst one year later, then advanced to a senior analyst 18 months later. This makes you look like a go-getter with the potential for leadership.

Pro tip: Don't neglect your online profile and resume, even if you have no plans of leaving your current company—keep them up to date. While many people think LinkedIn is the "most boring social network" around, it's extremely valuable in the professional world. You don't want to miss out on the opportunity for your dream job because you don't "appear" qualified. When you get promoted, update your title and position description as soon as you can.

Increased responsibilities

A promotion doesn't always come with a title change, but it will definitely come with more responsibilities. If you've proven to your superiors that you can be trusted and have the talent and capacity to do more, you'll notice an uptick in your job duties

For instance, imagine you're a sales manager who has been with your company for one and a half years. Your boss comes to you and says, "Steve, you've demonstrated great work by surpassing your sales quota over the last two quarters. We're going to double the coverage of the territory you're responsible for from $5 million to $10 million. You'll have the opportunity to make more money in commission, and you'll get a base raise in salary as well." This increase in responsibilities is a promotion, even if your title hasn't changed.

Some other examples of increased responsibility without a title change include:

- Getting bigger, more valuable client accounts
- Expanding the amount of staff you supervise and train

- Acquiring responsibility for selling multiple product lines

Even if you keep the same title for several years, create separate entries on your resume or professional online portfolio each time you are given a substantial increase in job duties. Recording your responsibilities this way makes it easier for hiring managers and recruiters to take notice of your career development.

For example, say you are a sales manager for a leading software company. Without changing your title, the company increases your coverage area from a $5 million territory to a $10 million territory. This is a huge step up in responsibilities, with potential for you to manage more sales and clients, increase the company's revenue, and earn higher commissions. Here's how you should record this advancement on your resume:

Sales Manager – Mid-Atlantic Region (2017-present)
- Promoted to oversee $10 million sales territory
- Increased territory sales to $12 million within 10 months

Sales Manager – East Division (2015-2017)
- Oversaw $5 million sales territory and ranked as #1 sales manager

Pro tip: If you've received a promotion without a title change a few times, you can always ask for an updated title if you really want one. The worst thing your boss can say is no. For example, if you're a Sales Manager who

> starts managing a large group of sales reps, ask for a title such as "Senior Sales Manager" or "Supervisory Sales Manager."

ADDITIONAL PERKS

New titles, a better salary, and more responsibilities aren't the only signs you're being recognized at work. The corporate world has numerous other bells and whistles to acknowledge that you're moving up in the organization and encourage high performance.

Supplementary compensation

Awarding a higher base salary isn't the only way companies reward top achievers. Many organizations will provide a higher annual bonus if you've exceeded expectations and added significant value to the bottom line at the end of the year.

You might not even have to wait until year's end to reap the financial benefits of your hard work. Some companies permit separate merit or performance-based bonuses on a quarterly basis—or any time supervisors deem appropriate.

Other financial incentives that frequently go along with promotions include things like stock options or an increase in your 401(k) matching program.

More power

Power in the workplace is a meaningful motivator for some professionals. Many people thrive on increased power, and it's often woven into job promotions. Smart bosses are able to discern who will use power to help others increase productivity and grow.

Getting an increase in power can manifest itself in a variety of ways. It could mean managing more direct reports or being in charge of training new hires. Or, you could be given an administrative assistant or shared coordinator, allowing you to shed some menial work on your plate and focus on more important business. You could also gain power by being invited to higher level meetings and workgroups where decisions are being made and your voice will be heard.

Work environment and lifestyle perks

There are a variety of methods companies use to reward high performers that don't necessarily cost much, but go a long way toward improving employee satisfaction. For example, your organization could move you from a cubicle where you have to listen to other people banter all day to a private office with a door you can close.

Successful employees with proven track records also earn high levels of trust. You might be given a company car with its own company-paid insurance policy. You could be granted flexible work hours or the option to work from home on certain days. If your supervisor can count on your to get your work done, they will likely let you do it on your own terms.

It's common for companies to give workers additional vacation time and personal days with each year of service.

However, some organizations leverage the power of time off work to reward top performers. A promotion package can include an extra week of paid time off, or personal days you can cash in at your convenience. Some progressive companies even go as far as rewarding their best employees with a pre-planned paid vacation and announcing it company-wide.

The bottom line? Smart companies do what it takes to reward their team members who deserve a promotion. Doing so fosters a positive organizational cultures, increases morale and employee motivation, and decreases costly turnover.

KEY TAKEAWAYS

- People get promoted for a variety of reasons. Your job is to take it seriously, step up to the plate, and showcase your potential in order to advance your career.
- You can get promoted without a change in title. Don't forget to record your increases in responsibility on your resume and professional online profile.
- An increased base salary and updated title aren't the only way to reflect a promotion. You can reap the benefits of additional compensation through bonuses and stock options.
- Power, authority, and lifestyle perks are also influential factors that come along with promotions.

CHAPTER 2.

CAN YOU GET A RAISE WITHOUT A PROMOTION?

Most promotions come with a raise—because they come with added responsibilities. However, raises can be different and separate from promotions.

The amount of money you earn is your lifeblood—it pays your bills and funds your chosen lifestyle. In 2015, a Mercer study found that the amount of money an employee makes is the most valued aspect of their job, but only 55% of workers are satisfied with their wages.

In this chapter, you'll learn about the different forms of raises in the business world—and strategies for how to get them.

ANNUAL RAISES: SHOULD I EXPECT A RAISE EVERY YEAR?

Usually, you should expect a raise every year. Most organizations recognize that an annual bump in employees' pay rate is necessary to retain top talent and keep up with inflation—and this type of pay increase is separate and distinct from raises you get for high performance. If you aren't getting a small raise every year, you should talk to your boss to find out why. Standard annual raises usually average around 2-4%.

What does it mean to keep up with inflation or the cost of living? For example, the rate of inflation in 2018 hovered around 2%. That means you're paying 2% more for everything than the year before—your rent or mortgage, car, groceries, entertainment—you get the gist. If your salary isn't keeping up with the rise in your cost of living, you're technically making less money than the year before.

Pro tip: When unemployment is low, it's an employee's market. More people are leaving organizations voluntarily to change jobs or embrace self-employment. The most competitive businesses respond by stretching annual raises to 5% or more to retain top talent.

Of course, there are always exceptions. For example, maybe the company you work for is in a financial crisis and temporarily freezes annual raises for all employees until the business recovers. Or, imagine you work at a promising startup that's running on a shoestring budget. You might not receive yearly raises for the first few years, but you could earn stock as a percentage of the company—potentially reaping huge rewards down the road when the business is acquired.

SALARY ADJUSTMENTS OR "CATCH-UP" RAISES

Salary adjustments are often known as "catch-up" raises. They are different than promotions because you usually won't get a new title—but they often have the same effect on your paycheck.

Your pay may be lagging behind your peers for a variety of reasons. Maybe you've been at the company for a long time and have only received small annual increases. Perhaps you accepted an offer with a low salary while your coworkers negotiated higher pay—but even with healthy annual raises every year, you're still making well below your market value.

For example, imagine you started your career with the company five years ago as an accountant with a salary of $45,000—and you accepted the offer without negotiating for higher pay. Each year you've received a 3% raise, and after five years, you're still making under $52,000. However, the market has shifted over time, and new hires with five years of accounting experience are now offered a salary of $57,000. Your new coworker, Reese, negotiated a starting salary of $60,000. He's at least $8,000 ahead of you even though you've exhibited top performance.

It's up to you to bring up your salary adjustment with your boss. As we'll discuss throughout this book, no one cares about your career and financial status more than you. You can make the argument that you shouldn't be penalized for staying with the company for a long time. Loyalty to a company should be recognized and rewarded. You still deserve to be earning as much as your colleagues in similar positions. If you present a strong case, an excellent boss will go to bat for you to get your salary in line with your peers, experience, and performance.

> **Pro tip**: Point out that raises based on performance and value should be completely separate from annual increases—and that you should be able to receive both at the same time. For instance, suppose you're earning $50,000 per year and you typically receive a 4% raise. This year, you ask for an 18% salary adjustment increase. If you get it, you should still receive your 4% annual raise on top of the salary adjustment.

THE MOST EFFECTIVE WAY TO GET A SIGNIFICANT RAISE: CHANGE JOBS

The fastest way to get a big bump in your salary is to change jobs entirely.

How do you know if leaving the organization for a new role is the right move? First, look at how much more money you're being offered. The average raise an employee receives when leaving for a new job is a 10-20% salary increase.

For example, assume you've been a marketing specialist with an advertising agency for almost two years. You started out with a salary of $48,500 and got an annual raise of 3% last year, bumping you up to almost $50,000. Then you receive an offer from another company to join their team as a digital marketing manager. It comes with more responsibility and a $60,000 salary—a 20% raise.

Should you accept? There are several factors to consider—don't look at the tempting paycheck alone. Does the new company offer better or similar time off and insurance policies? Are there other desirable perks (or a lack thereof)?

Is it an excellent place to work that values their employees? Explore the kind of reputation the company's culture has online via various review sites—the grass isn't always greener on the other side.

> **Pro tip**: You can ask these questions during the interview process. Moreover, progressive companies will include separate conversations with employees who would be your equals to give you a thorough understanding of their culture and whether you'd be a good fit.

Of course, you don't have to leave the organization to get a large raise quickly—we will dive deeper into the topic of getting promoted with the same company in the rest of this book. In fact, staying loyal to your company can pay off in the long run with more promotions and a bigger paycheck.

KEY TAKEAWAYS

- While raises and promotions both usually mean more money in your pocket, they aren't the same thing.
- Annual raises are meant to keep up with the rate of inflation—they're different from merit or performance-based raises.
- There are several reasons why you may have fallen behind the average market pay in your current salary. Be your own advocate and gather the right information to make the case for a "catch-up" adjustment raise.
- One way to get a significant raise is to get a new job. Look at all the factors outside of salary before

making a big move. And remember, you don't have to leave to get a substantial raise—it's often best to focus on getting a promotion at your current organization!

CHAPTER 3.

WHY IS GETTING PROMOTED IMPORTANT?

Getting promoted is much more than receiving a new title—it's a milestone that improves your financial status, impacts your work relationships, boosts your resume, and keeps your career interesting.

THE COMPOUNDING EFFECT: HOW PROMOTION INFLUENCES YOUR EARNINGS

Albert Einstein once said, "The most powerful force in the universe is compound interest." Benjamin Franklin said it well in his own words: "The money that money earns, earns money."

Consider this striking analogy: imagine someone asked you if you'd rather be given a million dollars in one month or one penny that was doubled every day for 30 days. What would you choose? Amazingly, when you double the penny every day for 30 days, you end up with over five times more than the first option of one million dollars—the pennies add up to $5,368,709.12 on day 30.

The effect of compounding has a similar impact on your career—that's why getting promoted (and the raises that come with it) is so important to your earning potential. For example, if you start out with a low salary and only receive meager 2-4% annual increases, you'll be *way* behind your peers in just a few years.

Imagine two 25-year-olds, Bart and Lisa. They start their careers as data analysts at a finance company. Bart has a starting salary of $60,000 and Lisa negotiates a salary of $65,000. If they both received 3% annual raises without promotions, Lisa would earn $377,000 more than Bart over the course of a 40-year career.

When you factor in the power of promotions, the difference in their earnings grows exponentially. Assume Bart is stagnant in his career and never gets promoted. Lisa, on the other hand, gets a promotion about every two years with an average salary bump of 6%—along with her 3% annual cost-of-living raise. The difference in their 40-year earnings is now astronomical: Lisa will earn $1.77 million more than Bart.

The bottom line? Promotions and raises have a tremendous impact on your financial future. Negotiate your starting salary *and* put in the work to earn regular promotions. You'll learn more about the best strategies and steps you can take to get a promotion in the upcoming chapters of this book.

PROMOTIONS ENHANCE YOUR RESUME

Think of your resume as your "elevator pitch." It doesn't merely summarize your experience and education—it represents your professional brand and helps you stand out from the competition. When one or two sheets of paper reflect your expertise and capabilities, you need to make every word count.

A hiring manager or recruiter doesn't know you personally. They have to decide if you're a candidate worthy of an interview based on a snapshot of your career. If your resume reflects long periods of time where you're stuck in the same position, you won't look promising to potential future employers because you've haven't advanced. They will wonder why you've been at the same level for a long time without any movement—and likely move on to other applicants.

In the same vein, assume you've moved around to various companies but have always held a similar title and duties. Lateral moves don't suggest you're ready to take on more responsibilities and a more advanced title. For example, if the last three jobs on your resume have comparable titles such as "client manager," it will look like you've become stagnant even if you've taken on increased responsibilities over time.

Make sure your resume includes any added job responsibilities in each role, even if you didn't get a raise or formal promotion. Some relevant examples include:

- Managing more employees
- Taking on an expanded sales territory
- Interviewing job candidates
- Onboarding or training new hires

However, there's one caveat: there may be times where your personal circumstances create a situation where a lateral move makes the most sense. For instance, maybe you're a working parent focused on making sure you have enough time to spend with your children. Be sure to tell potential employers your goals and ambitions—great companies respect a variety of lifestyles, and it helps both of you determine if a new role is the right fit.

> **Pro tip**: When you can, include success metrics in your resume. For example, if your marketing campaign generated three times the number of converted leads as expected, don't be humble—include it in the "major accomplishments" section of your position description.

DON'T GET TAKEN FOR GRANTED

If you fall into a comfortable role at work where your boss can trust and rely on you but also doesn't have to reward you, you risk getting taken for granted. It's not even necessarily intentional—it happens all the time in relationships, friendships, and families.

Many boss-employee relationships can fall into this pattern if you aren't careful. You need to be an advocate for your career and talent. Don't get taken advantage of because you're good at your job. Without being grandiose, remind your boss of your accomplishments and that you expect to be rewarded for high performance.

Establish a habit of letting your supervisor know you want to move up in the organization. When you ask for a promotion, you don't want to hear your boss say, "Oh, I thought you were happy here as a junior account executive—you're great at it and I like having you here. You never said anything before."

It's all about setting expectations and maintaining robust communication that prevents you from getting stuck in your career advancement journey. We'll dig deeper into the specific tactics in later chapters, but staying on your boss' radar is paramount to getting the results you want—so when you ask for a promotion, he won't be surprised.

OPPORTUNITIES FOR PERSONAL GROWTH AND NEW CHALLENGES

You probably wouldn't be reading this book if you weren't invested in your own personal development. Most human beings are interested in growing as people and embarking on new challenges—it feels good! Otherwise, jobs can get boring and extremely soul-draining. One of the fastest ways to become stagnant in your job is by getting bored with your daily work—or getting too complacent to suggest improvements.

For example, imagine you're a human resources associate and you spend most of your time scanning resumes for quality job candidates. The work is tedious, but you have innovative ideas for how to improve it—like inviting applicants to stand out by sending in video cover letters, or using new software to find the best candidates.

Don't wait to be asked for your opinion—someone else will beat you to it! Make your passion for growing professionally a part of your campaign for getting promoted. Let your boss know what you're most interested in and the particular challenges you'd like to tackle. A stellar boss will admire your tenacity and respect your thorough communication.

KEY TAKEAWAYS

- Don't underestimate the power of the compounding effect on your potential earnings. Negotiating a robust starting salary and getting regular promotions will have an immense impact on your financial future.

- Promotions and increased responsibilities have a major impact on your resume—which doubles as your professional brand. Don't forget to include them even if you don't receive a new title.

- Ensure you don't fall into a comfortable role at work that leaves you getting taken for granted. Engage your boss in regular conversations about your desire to advance within the company.

- Promotions in your career also serve as an avenue for self-development, lifelong learning, and embracing new challenges.

CHAPTER 4.

EXCEL IN YOUR CURRENT ROLE

While you may be eager to earn a promotion, it's essential to take one thing at a time. That starts with being laser-focused on exhibiting high performance in your current role. Remember, if you're not shining in your position, you not only risk being passed up for a promotion, you could put your present job in danger.

WHY BEING GREAT AT YOUR JOB IS ESSENTIAL

Advancing your career doesn't happen overnight. Every person must gain the trust of their supervisors and colleagues to earn a well-deserved promotion. That means proving you're worthy of getting promoted by consistently exceeding expectations. Here are seven tips for excelling in your job every day.

Be engaged

When you're invested in your work, your boss (and their boss) notice. So, how does an engaged employee act? Engaged, motivated workers do more than attend every required meeting and show up to work on time. They often are the first ones to get to the office and the last ones to leave—many times taking work home with them in the evening or weekends.

High performers take workplace engagement to the next level. Arrive at meetings prepared with solutions rather than problems. Volunteer for new responsibilities that aren't listed in your job description. Contribute innovative ideas, and challenge the status quo. Even participating in voluntary professional development and attending office holiday parties and other celebrations demonstrate a commitment to the organizational culture.

Demonstrate pride in your work

Do your colleagues view you as someone with a strong work ethic who is proud of their work? Do you take ownership of projects from beginning to end, or do you have great ideas that are never fully realized? Do you proofread your emails and presentations before others see them?

Employees who are sincerely proud of the work they produce hate the idea of letting a project go unfinished or neglecting to correct careless errors. Everyone makes mistakes sometimes, but if you consistently show enthusiasm for generating exceptional work, people will take note. Don't forget to own your mistakes the same way do your successes. Taking the fall when you mess up and finding a solution illustrates humility and leadership potential.

Limit multi-tasking

Do you find yourself having 18 browser tabs open, answering the phone, and composing a text message at the same time? Our digital world makes it more tempting than ever to think we can get more done by doing several things at the same time. It's a common myth that multi-tasking increases productivity, but a 2009 Harvard study found that heavy multitaskers have decreased attention spans and unorganized workflows.

Fortunately, it's easy to develop habits that allow you to focus on one thing at a time. Create a prioritized to-do list at the start of the day and don't begin a new task until you've completed the prior one. When you're finished with a website, close it. Bookmark the sites you need to visit often. Give yourself two 15-minute periods to check and respond to emails each day.

Be a team player

There's no better way to shine at work than being an excellent team player. Successfully delivering on individual projects is great, but showing that you can lead and inspire a team is even better. Even if your particular position doesn't involve much teamwork, find creative ways to prove you can encourage your coworkers—and help them become better at their jobs.

For example, imagine the head of marketing, Bailie, is overseeing the development of a new company website. She wants feedback from a member of each department. Be the first to let Bailie know you're eager to participate. Research the best websites from the top companies in your industry and bring your ideas to the table. After all, helping your company raise its online profile is a valuable asset.

Become indispensable

What would your boss do if you resigned tomorrow? Would they promptly wish you well and congratulate you on your next endeavor, or would they try to persuade you to stay? In light of the competitive marketplace, superior talent is hard to discover and retain. If your boss views you as indispensable, they will do whatever they can in their power to keep you on board.

While it's standard advice to become indispensable at any organization, there's a caveat. You *should* strive to become irreplaceable to the company at large. However, it's your talent, attitude, and work ethic that should be indispensable—not your value in your current position.

Don't get pigeon-holed in your job by being the only one who is able to do it well. As you expand your own skillset at work, help others grow by teaching them how to do aspects of your job. Build your reputation as an asset to your company outside of your current role by being reliable, trustworthy, innovative, and forward-thinking. Exhibit those qualities in every interaction.

Attitude is everything

Think about the different personalities and perspectives you've seen at work. Have you ever worked with someone who brings a pessimistic outlook to the office every day? Even if the person is talented and intelligent, their attitude can impact the whole team. Negative attitudes spread quickly—contributing to toxic company culture, decreased productivity, and turnover.

The good news? Positive attitudes are just as contagious. If you want to climb the corporate ladder, smile and display a cheerful demeanor, especially in times of high stress or challenges. Doing so sets you apart as a leader who encourages others, can handle adversity, and brings positive energy to the workplace every day.

Keep it drama-free

Nearly everyone has seen what engaging in office politics and gossip can do to a work environment. It can turn a friendly professional atmosphere into a high school cafeteria with rumors, bullying, and distrust. The office becomes an unbearable place to work—projects get compromised, team morale dissolves, colleagues blame one another, and top workers start looking for new opportunities.

Being drama-free doesn't mean you have to like everyone you work with on a personal level. Inevitably, you'll have to collaborate with those who bring different personalities, work styles, and opinions to the table. Unless someone is harassing you or making it extremely difficult to do your job well, avoid any temptation to gossip or create office politics. It won't move you toward a promotion any faster.

HOW TO DETERMINE IF YOU'RE PERFORMING WELL

Now that you have strategies for shining in your current role, how can you tell if your efforts are working? The first step is knowing how to objectively tell if you're doing well with quantifiable results. For example, if you work in sales, it's easy to see if you're falling short of your quota or knocking it out of the park. If you work in information technology, you could measure the number of customer requests you've completed, new tools adopted, or technology availability rates.

Here are some strategies for keeping a pulse on your job performance.

Review your job description

Go back to the original job description you received when you were hired. Take a look at each of the main objectives and goals for your position. Are you doing those things? More importantly, are you doing them well?

Use those key goals and objectives to guide your performance plan. Make sure you are fulfilling all of your primary responsibilities. If there are any parts of your job that you don't have the resources or training to accomplish, bring it up to your boss so you can bridge the gap. They will appreciate you being proactive rather than waiting to explain why you didn't do it at your performance review.

Analyze your 360-degree feedback

360-degree feedback involves performance feedback from every type of person you encounter at work, such as supervisors, coworkers, stakeholders, and customers. Do you get rave reviews and recommendations from clients or vendors consistently? Do fellow team members praise your contributions to group projects? Did your boss' supervisor commend you on spearheading a new product design?

Keep a running portfolio of your successes, praise from colleagues, and messages from satisfied customers. Many employees do excellent work daily and go unrecognized because their supervisors don't know. While humility is essential, a moderate level of self-promotion is necessary to ensure your value is recognized.

Are recruiters reaching out?

If recruiters are contacting you about new opportunities, your hard work may be getting noticed. However, many recruiters contact lots of people, especially if your particular skillset is in high demand. Even if you are committed to advancing your career at your current company, you can still use offers from recruiters to your advantage.

Keep track of communications you receive from recruiters. If your supervisor realizes your skills are in high demand, your value gives you some leverage. If your boss knows there's competition for your talent, they are more willing to do whatever it takes to keep you on board.

Increased responsibilities and autonomy

One surefire way to tell if you're a high-performer is receiving increased responsibilities and the freedom to get your work done the way you see fit. While it may be stressful to take on a higher workload, view it as a sign that your boss respects your work and believes you're up for the challenge. Good supervisors won't give more work to employees they don't trust or have the confidence they can do it well.

Increased autonomy indicates your supervisor knows they don't have to micromanage you because you are reliable—

they trust your judgment and know you'll get the job done. Keep in mind that doesn't mean you can't ask for clarification or more detailed instructions. It's better to ask than produce work that falls short because you didn't fully understand what was needed.

KEY TAKEAWAYS

- Before you focus on getting a promotion, prove you are indispensable to the organization by becoming an engaged, collaborative asset.
- Get noticed by showing pride in your work, being a team player, and having a positive attitude every day.
- Avoid the temptation of office politics, gossip, and workplace drama. It won't help your career and it *will* contribute to toxic company culture.
- Proactively measure your performance to validate your contributions at work. Share your successes with your boss regularly.
- Don't hesitate to ask your boss for feedback and guidance. A good boss is committed to helping you become better at your job.

CHAPTER 5.

PROVE YOU'RE READY FOR THE NEXT STEP

Now that you have the strategies to make sure you're doing your current job well, it's time to zoom in on showing your boss you're ready to level up to the next stage. After all, being good at your job is one thing, but proving you're worthy of moving up the ladder requires a thoughtful game plan.

HOW DO YOU SHOW YOU'RE READY TO MOVE UP?

Your boss knows you're good at your job. You're reliable, trustworthy, and you're consistently exceeding expectations. However, if you want a promotion, you need to be an advocate for your own career advancement. Here are some ways to demonstrate that you're prime promotion material.

Always be learning

If you aren't continually learning, you'll become stagnant and fall behind. Salespeople operate under the mantra, "ABC—Always Be Closing." When working toward a promotion, adopt an "ABL—Always be Learning" mindset. A commitment to lifelong learning is what turns you into a better version of yourself every day.

That improved version of yourself is not only what makes you better at your job, it also drives business results. If you want to be considered for a promotion, generating impressive results is a great way to go. Don't forget to keep a running log of each learning opportunity you participate in. When your supervisor asks about your professional development efforts, you'll have a robust list ready.

There's no shortage of professional and personal learning opportunities available. Sign up for webinars related to your industry or position, attend conferences, and read books that improve your knowledge base.

Pro tip: Ask your human resources team if the company has a professional development stipend—many progressive businesses allocate $500 or more per year to help their employees grow. Even if you spend money out-of-pocket on professional development, it's often tax-deductible.

Take initiative

All that learning becomes diluted without taking the initiative to put your knowledge into action. Project yourself as a go-getter by taking initiative rather than expecting that opportunities for you to shine will fall in your lap. Boldly taking the initiative without being told what to do also fosters the trust of your boss while making their life easier.

You might feel timid at first, but don't be afraid to speak up if you have a great idea. Imagine if you kept silent about a marketing strategy that could double inbound leads during a team meeting. One of your colleagues takes the floor and presents the approach in their own words.

They get the credit, but you'll have missed out because you didn't seize the opportunity.

Not every idea is going to be an exceptional one, but if you never voice them, you won't stand out. Plus, speaking up has little downside. Unless your idea is truly dreadful (like suggesting everyone wear a specific color each day), it will be forgotten quickly. It's the great ideas that people remember!

Be a problem solver

No one likes problems, so what better way to position yourself for promotion than being someone who's counted on to deliver innovative solutions? In today's digital world, things move fast and change is constant. Be an excellent problem-solver by anticipating change and developing proactive solutions.

Excellent problem-solving skills require you to be a good communicator. Whenever there's an issue to resolve, it's essential to remember that you can't please everyone. Help your colleagues understand the problem, validate each individual's point of view, and craft several solutions. Enlist the help of your coworkers to identify which solution is the best fit. By leading the problem-solving process, you indicate you have the leadership skills necessary for a promotion.

For instance, imagine team morale is low in your department. Talk with each member of the team to discover the causes. Tom says he feels left out of decisions, Sam doesn't think team members trust one another, and Savannah feels no one ever asks for her opinion. Help solve the problem by engaging the department in activities that build rapport and trust. You could establish a collaborative online workspace to increase communication and transparency, work with the team to create departmental core values, and even plan monthly social outings.

Know when to delegate

The saying, "If you want it done right, do it yourself" doesn't work when you're trying to get ahead in the business world. It's tempting, but doing every task your way doesn't make the best use of your skills. Successful professionals leverage the knowledge and skills of their colleagues—and they exhibit the authority to hold others accountable.

Insisting on doing everything yourself also creates bottlenecks in the team workflow. For example, if you're the only one who can approve a vendor order, what happens if you're out sick or swamped with other tasks? The action item goes untouched, deadlines get missed, and the blame falls on you.

Furthermore, if you ostracize other team members and refuse to let them take on meaningful work, you risk gaining a reputation as a control freak—and you're likely to burn out. There will always be times where you need to take charge of a project, but the smartest employees know how to recognize the skills of teammates and delegate appropriately.

Make your boss look good

Is there a more effective way to get noticed than helping your boss prove they're doing a great job? When you know your supervisor has a full plate, offer to take some tasks on yourself—before they ask. You'll make their workload more manageable and gain the opportunity to show them how well you perform.

For example, if your boss needs to reschedule your weekly one-on-one check-in because they're too busy, ask how you can lighten their load. If you know they have an executive meeting or a significant project with a quick deadline, offer to proofread their presentation. If they are slammed with expense reports but have also been tasked with finding a new vendor, propose contacting vendors to get the information they need. A good supervisor will be thrilled that you're willing to pitch in and will recognize your dedication.

Look the part

Remember the famous mottos, "image is everything" and "dress for the job you want"? While your work performance doesn't have much to do with how you dress, people still place importance on a professional appearance. You don't have to break the bank filling your closet with expensive clothes—just be sensible.

You can still stay true to your sense of fashion. If you prefer bright colors, go for it—just keep mixed patterns under control. If you look like you should have a Geek Squad lanyard around your neck ready to assist customers at Best

Buy, think about a style upgrade. Look at the executives in your office. You don't have to mimic them, but it gives you a good idea of what's expected.

The bottom line—arrive to work well-groomed and dressed appropriately. Beyond that, focus on putting your work ethic in the forefront.

START DOING THE JOB OR GET THE PROMOTION FIRST?

Should you start doing the job you want before you're promoted, or wait until you receive the promotion? It's a classic "chicken or the egg" question. There's no one right answer, but there are several aspects you should consider before you decide.

The safest method: overperforming

Going above and beyond your job description may be the safest way to earn a promotion. Get out of your comfort zone and prove you have what it takes to handle increased responsibility. However, just because you start tackling more advanced work doesn't mean you'll be automatically promoted.

Your boss may be thinking, "Show me you're ready for a promotion by proving you can do the job you want." It may feel tedious to undertake more responsibilities and work longer hours without an increase in pay, but it will pay off. Remember, make sure you document your added duties so you can present a sound case for your promotion when the time is right.

Risks of automatically overachieving

In some companies, doing things that haven't explicitly been assigned to you can be viewed as overstepping boundaries. It can even result in conflicts with other team members and duplicated work if proper communication isn't in place.

For example, imagine you've crafted a new onboarding strategy for the company's client ambassador program. You're excited to present your vision at the next team meeting, but when you do, your colleague becomes upset. She's been working on the same thing for the last month— with your boss' permission. You end up looking like you aren't focused on your current job duties, and you've stepped on your coworker's toes.

If you expect your efforts to overachieve won't send the right message, concentrate on working smarter, not harder. As you learned in the last chapter, excelling in your current role gives you an abundance of opportunities to shine. If you're too focused on doing things outside of your job description, you could be wasting your time. Spend that time and energy on other areas that propel your career forward, such as professional development and networking.

Consider company culture and history

Company culture and historical internal promotion policies play a big part in your strategy. Do some research to uncover how decisions are made in your organization. Do you see others being promoted when they start doing the job they want first, or because they performed well in a previous position?

While your research will undoubtedly reveal some clues, it's also beneficial to reach out to your supervisor and other coworkers. Ask your boss how they got promoted. Did they start doing the job first or did they wait? It's possible they will expect you to advance the same way. Plus, a good boss will value your open communication and understand that you're interested in moving up.

Additionally, consider having a conversation with someone from your human resources department or talent development team. They are there to help you succeed and grow. They'll likely educate you on the company's promotional pathways and offer tips to get ahead. Keep in mind that it's not just your immediate supervisor who's in control of when you get promoted. Developing positive relationships with people in all areas of your organization positions you as a valuable asset who's ready for the next step.

KEY TAKEAWAYS

- Proving you're ready for the next step in your career requires initiative and problem-solving skills.
- Trying to do everything yourself won't win you any points. To stand out, exhibit your ability to delegate appropriately.
- Make things easier for your boss. It shows you don't need to be micromanaged and can be trusted to take on more responsibilities.

- Before you start automatically overachieving, communicate with your boss. Don't risk duplicating work or overstepping bounds by not asking.
- Understand your company's promotion pathways and develop relationships with coworkers at all levels of the organization.

CHAPTER 6.

HOW TO GET
NOTICED AT WORK

Wouldn't it be great if hard work were enough to secure a promotion? Don't fall into the trap of thinking that's all it takes—it's an illusion. In today's competitive atmosphere, a strong work ethic isn't always its own reward. You have to get noticed by the decision-makers in your organization if you want your efforts to pay off.

THE BEST WAYS TO ENSURE YOUR BOSS NOTICES YOU

It's crucial to realize that your boss isn't necessarily focused on you all the time. While most people are raised to be humble and avoid bragging, it's okay to bring your accomplishments to your boss' attention. Don't think of it as self-promotion, think of it as being your own advocate— and ensuring you get recognized for your contributions. Earn a better title and a more substantial paycheck by making sure your company acknowledges the value you bring to the table.

Polish your networking skills

You need to do more than show up and get your work done on time. You must be present and network with others in the organization. If you choose to stay under the radar, you become invisible—and invisible employees don't land promotions. It also demonstrates a lack of engagement and poor professional social skills.

Exceptional networkers are very likable. In fact, a 2008 study by Cornell University researchers found that the value placed on an employee's competence varies depending on how well they are liked. Don't dismiss the importance of networking in and out of the office—or associate it with schmoozing, gossip, or office politics.

Remember, effective networking doesn't mean you have to endlessly self-promote yourself. It involves fostering authentic, genuine relationships with your colleagues. Positively engaging with others helps you stand out from the crowd.

For example, if you're picking up coffee, offer to order one for your coworker. Participate in work-related extracurricular activities, such as recreational sports teams or holiday parties. Even better, plan an office potluck or start a book club. Networking possibilities are limitless—it's up to you! You may even have fun and benefit personally from new friendships outside of work.

Pro tip: If you feel like you have to be fake or engage in office politics in order to get along with others, it could be a sign of a corporate culture that just doesn't match your personality. It may be time to re-assess whether the company is a good fit.

Provide value outside of your department

Don't get stuck in your current position by neglecting to show you're capable of getting out of your comfort zone. Use your skills and experiences to help your colleagues in other areas of the business succeed. If you impress people in various departments with your creativity and collaboration, your boss will hear about your work ethic. You will show that you can take ownership of your own role *and* provide value to other teams—thus demonstrating your investment in the broader mission and vision of the company.

For instance, If you work in the finance department and you strike up a conversation with someone at the grocery store who could be a potential client, don't keep it to yourself. Give the prospect some information on your company's offerings and ask permission to pass on their contact information to a colleague in sales.

> **Pro tip**: Keep in mind that your contributions should support the company's bottom line. If you generate revenue or new business, you'll always be viewed as a powerful asset.

Associate with the "A-team"

You are the company you keep, so be mindful of who you spend time with at work. The last thing you want is to be associated with those who do the bare minimum on the job. Don't hang out around the water cooler chatting with the "cool kids" who treat work like a popularity contest. They don't take their jobs seriously—just like the kids in high school who were too busy skipping class and crafting senior pranks to focus on getting good grades.

Get noticed by standing next to the known superstars in the organization. Put your ego aside and seek out colleagues who have more experience and knowledge than you. You'll learn what it takes to get ahead and form powerful allies company-wide.

If you surround yourself with the right people, you'll be more confident in your job and perform better. Striving to keep up with the "team" also amplifies your natural competitive energy and pushes you to reach stretch goals. Great colleagues want to help you boost your own career and succeed in tandem.

And, when you associate with other high achievers, you'll be exposed to more advancement opportunities. For example, say your coworker Joe mentions an internal opening over lunch in the company cafeteria one day. He's not interested in the job, but it sounds like a great fit for you.

> **Pro tip**: Invite a star employee to lunch to learn about their career path. Or, if you discover you and a top performer have a shared interest, such as golfing or running, ask them to join you.

Find an excellent mentor

Seeking a mentor within the company gives you a powerful advantage, especially if you're young or just starting out in your career. The best mentors are like guardian angels, serving as a sounding board, offering valuable advice, and helping you hone your skills. A great mentor will also provide insight and knowledge into upper-level company politics that would take years for you to attain on your own.

For example, imagine you're frustrated because your coworker, Jim, is slacking on the job and it's increasing your workload. You end up skipping lunch and staying late a few times a week. It's tempting to complain to your boss, but you don't want to look like a whiny tattletale. Ask your mentor how to handle the situation best. They will know the proper action you should take to solve the issue without damaging your reputation.

Don't be afraid to ask someone to be your mentor. Most successful professionals recall their own past mentors who helped them navigate the often choppy waters of the corporate world. A good mentor will be honored that you asked and eager to share their knowledge, help you grow, and showcase your talent to get ahead.

> **Pro tip**: Mentors who have a good working relationship with your boss, your boss' supervisor, or even future bosses—and see your potential—become enormous advocates for your upward growth in the long term.

Become an expert in your industry

Knowledge is power. To get noticed, position yourself as a thought leader in your field. Keep a pulse on the latest news and trends in your industry and bring them up with coworkers—and your manager. Sign up for the newsletters from the major publications in your line of work. Leverage a program such as Google News to receive alerts aligned to your business. Join online and in-person discussion groups related to your work.

When you find something interesting that could have an impact on the company, email it your boss, or even leave it on their desk with a note about why it's relevant. It exhibits passion and dedication to your job—and that you're thinking ahead to help the company develop a strategic response.

Another way to get recognized as an industry expert across the organization is to utilize your research to prepare for meetings. For example, say you're in the marketing department and you have an upcoming meeting about maximizing the reach of your social media channels. Research current trends and what your competitors are doing. Show up to the meeting with a detailed report, your recommendations, and your sources. When the floor is open for input, you'll be poised to show you've done your homework and are able to offer tangible solutions.

Work for an outstanding boss

Working for a robust leader is the foundation for becoming a great leader. If you are lucky enough to have one, a great boss makes it much easier to advance within the company. You won't usually get to choose your supervisor, but it's smart to know what to look out for during the interview process.

A great manager will be enthusiastic about helping you develop your skillset and advance to the next level. They will also be transparent and open to communication about upcoming job openings— and what you can do to earn them. The best bosses will give you ample training, meaningful feedback, and a plethora of chances to take the limelight.

KEY TAKEAWAYS

- Go beyond putting in the hours and producing great work. Network with others and participate in company events to get noticed.
- Demonstrate value outside of your department. Leverage every opportunity to generate revenue and new business for the organization.
- Foster a relationship with a great mentor—they'll be an advocate who gives you the support and knowledge that propels you to the next level.
- Associate with high-performing superstars in every layer of the organization.
- Work for a great boss. An excellent supervisor will be invested in your career and provide you with the training, tools, and resources to perform your best.
- Stand out as an industry expert. People notice the employee everyone goes to for information about what's happening in your field.

CHAPTER 7.

DOES YOUR BOSS KNOW YOU WANT A PROMOTION?

While getting noticed at work certainly enhances your reputation, it's critical to be specific with your boss about your desire to be promoted. You can't expect your supervisor to be a mind reader. If you don't explicitly tell them, how else would you expect them to be aware of your goals?

Don't let assumptions keep you from getting ahead. Remember, just because you're eager to be promoted doesn't mean everyone else wants the same thing. Promotions often come with increased responsibilities, more pressure, and longer hours. Some people are happy to stay in their current jobs for many reasons. For example, they may not want to manage other people, or they may want to ensure they maintain a good work-life balance.

ROUTINE CHECK-INS ARE YOUR SECRET WEAPON

Nearly every organization uses yearly performance reviews to appraise each employee's performance—but that's not enough if you're determined to get a promotion. You must initiate regular check-ins with your boss to review your performance, discuss your goals, and set mutually-agreed-upon expectations.

Identifying promotion-worthy performance

If you don't know what kind of behaviors and actions your supervisor deems worthy of a promotion, how can you effectively devise a plan that helps you get there? The key to routine check-ins is to discuss your career in a way that paves a path for an excellent review of your yearly performance.

About once per quarter, schedule a meeting with your boss. If you work in different locations and you don't get the opportunity to interact much outside of your check-ins, consider meeting more frequently. These meetings lay the groundwork for your performance review and career advancement. Ask them, "How am I doing? Am I exceeding your expectations? What else should I be doing to earn a promotion? When should I be accomplishing these tasks or goals?"

Document the feedback your boss gives you and use it as a roadmap for your career development. Utilize it to guide your next conversation, as well as your performance review. Create an outline of what your boss said you're doing well and what else you can do to improve. Record the action steps you take in response to their feedback. Then you'll have the evidence you need to state your case for promotion when the time is right.

For example, imagine you're a human resources specialist and your boss says you're doing a great job quickly assessing job candidates' qualifications. However, the HR team loses 50% of qualified candidates if an interview with the hiring manager isn't quickly scheduled. Your supervisor suggests crafting a solution for setting those interviews within 48 hours and presenting it at the next team meeting. After your presentation, you record your achievement on your outline, along with the completion date to show you hit the benchmark on time (the more data you have, the better your outline looks). Now you have written documentation of your performance, nicely packaged and ready to go for your next check-in or review.

> **Pro tip**: No one else will schedule check-ins for you, not even your boss. Unlike in high school, where you had a school career counselor to remind you what to do, you have to take it upon yourself in adulthood. It's your career—take the reins!

Your boss wants to hear from you

You might worry that setting regular check-ins shows you aren't being considerate of your boss' busy schedule—especially if you're early in your career. However, that's simply not true. A good boss *wants* to hear from you, mentor you, and help you reach your goals. Scheduling check-ins with your supervisor gives them confidence that you're invested in your career with the company and you're committed to moving up.

Human resources professionals often hear managers complain about workers who don't exhibit initiative or ownership for their own careers. For instance, envision a sales supervisor saying to an HR leader, "I have three sales representatives on my team who never bother to check in with me regarding their performance or ask what they can do to advance in the organization. Did you give me three employees on cruise control?"

You don't want to get a reputation as someone on autopilot at work, doing just enough to get by and riding the coattails of colleagues. Nor do you want to associate yourself with slacker employees who avoid difficult tasks and try to look busy so no one bothers them.

Avoid the risk of your boss perceiving you this way at all costs! Establishing an open, transparent dialogue about your goals and aspirations through regular meetings is paramount to your success. Your boss and your career will thank you for it in the long run.

Make check-in scheduling simple

How should you schedule the meetings? Go back to the principle of making things easier for your boss. Rather than shooting emails back and forth about a time that works, find an open slot on their calendar and send an invitation. Even better, use a scheduling tool in your calendar program that examines your schedules and allows your boss to choose when you meet. This gives your manager the control to pick a time that's most convenient for them when you're both available.

> **Pro tip**: A productive meeting doesn't equal a long meeting. Arrive prepared with two or three discussion topics. At the end, verbalize action items and expectations. Keep the meeting to 30 minutes or less—

> your boss will appreciate your thoughtful consideration
> of their time!

FREQUENCY OF CHECK-INS—AND WHY IT MATTERS

Make sure to toe the line carefully when planning your check-in meetings. Too many meetings can become bothersome to your boss and frame you as an employee that needs constant, repetitive feedback. You don't want your messages to end up in the "spam" inbox of your boss' mind.

Avoid scheduling a weekly recurring meeting—you'll both end up dreading your Wednesday afternoons. A good rule of thumb is every quarter. Remember, you still want to project autonomy and confidence. Talk with your boss to mutually decide what works best.

Lay groundwork with the rule of seven

The "Rule of Seven" is a classic sales and marketing psychology principle you can apply to earn a promotion. The rule advises that it takes at least seven exposures or touchpoints of a thought, idea, or product before someone considers making a purchase or adopting an idea.

Everyone is selling something. In your case, you're selling the idea that you're a valuable employee who should be promoted. Think of it as a long-term campaign or game plan for your career advancement. You're unlikely to make the "sale" the first time you mention it.

You're laying the groundwork months before you make your actual "ask." Similar to a salesperson fostering trust with a potential buyer, be patient and take your time. Keep in mind, the number seven is just a general guide—it's not set in stone. The underlying meaning is that your promotion campaign is a marathon, not a sprint. Focus on exposing your boss to the case for your promotion over time, building their trust and confidence with each touchpoint.

Each check-in is considered a touchpoint, so be sure to reveal your strengths and provide your boss with tangible examples of your accomplishments every time you meet. For instance, if you're on the legal team, point out that you overshot your client interactions goal by 20% during the last quarter. If you're on the sales team, highlight your quarterly success in converting 125% more qualified leads into customers than expected for your monthly quota. You'll organically build meaningful touchpoints that make the case for your promotion with every check-in.

Ensure the ask goes smoothly

By following the advice in this chapter, you are laying the foundation for a successful promotion pitch—so that when you're ready to ask the big question, you won't be coming in cold. Through your regular check-ins, you'll have established the proof you need to show you're deserving of moving up in the organization.

To calm your nerves, reference prior conversations with your boss. It's normal to be a bit anxious when asking for a promotion, but you've prepared for several months, so you're ready. You've communicated with your boss about what it will take to advance, and you've delivered results. Plus, your boss will likely see this conversation coming since you've been an avid advocate for yourself and documenting your achievements.

Have confidence that you've set the stage to receive the promotion you're prepared to ask for. Be calm and collected, so you won't be emotional. Don't forget, this isn't all about what you want, it's about what you've worked hard for and deserve.

KEY TAKEAWAYS

- Earning a promotion means you have to take ownership of your career path. Don't expect your boss to know you want to be promoted!
- Don't assume you know what your boss' expectations are. Ask, develop a plan, and document your achievements.
- Don't fall into the mindset of thinking you're bugging your boss by initiating regular check-ins. They want to hear from you—it's your secret weapon!
- It takes at least seven touchpoints for someone to get on board with an idea. Cultivate touchpoints into your long-term game plan.
- Don't schedule more than one check-in a month. You don't want to appear needy or unable to manage your work independently—make your meetings about assessing your performance and learning what you can do to get ahead.

CHAPTER 8.

HOW LONG SHOULD IT TAKE TO GET PROMOTED?

When you settle into your first corporate job, you probably ask yourself, "When should I get a promotion? How long does it take?" There are a plethora of factors that go into how long it takes to earn a promotion. Knowing what they are is the first step in advancing your career.

HOW TO GET YOUR TIMING RIGHT

How long it takes to get promoted depends on your industry and each individual company. Some companies advance workers faster or slower, but 18 months to two years is a standard expectation. Here are some timing considerations you should know about when seeking a promotion.

Avoid red flags in your professional background

If you've been in your current position for over two years, it's time to start assessing why you aren't advancing. When a recruiter or hiring manager looks at your resume and sees you've had the same title for two years or more, they often view it as a red flag.

A recruiter may wonder, "Why hasn't she moved up? Is there something wrong with her performance? Is she cruising along on autopilot?" Ideally, your experience should reflect that you've progressed into higher roles the longer you stay with a company, or that you left a company and accepted a more advanced position with a new organization.

However, not everyone's situation is ideal, and not everything is the same on paper as it is in reality. If you've had the same title for over two years, how do you explain why you haven't moved up?

Some jobs require highly specialized or technical roles. Describe your specific position and demonstrate that while your title hasn't changed, you've taken on increased responsibilities and your expertise and experience have deepened.

For example, imagine you're a sales representative, and your title hasn't changed in over two years. Explain that you've taken on new regional sales territories or have moved up from selling two product lines to four.

When to ask for a promotion

As you learned in the last chapter, you should be laying the groundwork for your promotion with a long-term campaign and regular check-ins. When it comes to the actual ask, timing is critical. Even if you and your boss agree you're ready for the promotion, asking at the wrong time can be a huge barrier.

There's a common misperception that your annual performance review is the right time and place to ask for a promotion. However, that's not how it works in most companies—they have regulated cycles for budgets, raises, and promotions. By the time annual employee appraisals are scheduled, promotion decisions have usually already been made.

Your boss' hands will likely be tied even if they want to promote you. A well-known complaint managers voice when an employee requests a promotion at their performance review is, "I wish I had known sooner. The budget is already locked."

Remedy this issue by conducting some research to get your finger on the pulse of the company's promotion and budget rhythm. There's no shortage of ways to get the right information. You can ask when you receive your job offer—your offer letter might even describe when candidates for promotion are evaluated. You can also always consult the human resources department, talk with your boss, or confer with colleagues who have worked at the company for several years.

Don't learn the hard way and miss your chance for a promotion because you didn't equip yourself with the proper knowledge. Start the conversation early and talk with your boss well in advance. Make the ask at least 30-60 days before your performance review to be considered for the promotion you desire.

> **Pro tip**: Initiating a proactive discussion concerning your career advancement will impress your boss. It shows him you're engaged and invested in moving forward.

HOW TO GET PROMOTED QUICKLY

Imagine you've been on the job for less than a year, but everything is going great and you're exceeding goals and expectations at every turn. You might be wondering, "How can I get promoted quickly?" It may be challenging to get promoted quickly, but it's certainly not impossible if the situation is right.

Job tenures get shorter every year, so rapid promotions are more prevalent than they were decades ago when people spent their entire careers at one company. Here are some key aspects to think about when you're aiming for a speedy promotion.

Consider your field or industry

The type of profession you have and the clients your company does business with have a significant impact on your potential for promotion. If you work in a stagnant organization, it can be hard to find growth avenues. However, if you work in a high-growth industry, there are plenty of reasons why you can move up faster than ever.

Take the technology field, for example. Technology advances every day, and so does the need for fresh talent. Many tech companies find they have to hire new employees at an alarming rate—creating the need to quickly find qualified people who can lead and manage new staff. Similarly, startup businesses typically scale quickly and must hire a fleet of new workers seemingly overnight.

Imagine you've been at a tech startup for nine months, and you're getting great feedback about your performance and valuable contributions. Your CEO hires 12 new web and mobile application developers—and posts for a new Technology Director position. You've only worked for the company for a short time, but you've demonstrated your ability and value. Ask your boss if he will consider you for the position. Startups often have a flat hierarchy and little red tape, making a swift advancement easier in some circumstances.

Even if you don't work in a high-growth industry where the demand for talent is increasing, your company's clients might be experiencing record growth. For instance, suppose you're an accountant, and your company represents a healthcare client who is preparing to hire 100 new employees.

They'll need more accounting support—and your boss suddenly needs a team lead for that account. You've been at the firm for 11 months, but you've been performing remarkably well and already created a long-term campaign for your promotion. Don't wait—ask him to recognize you as a candidate for the new role.

Choose the right boss

An exceptional boss does more than be available to listen and give you feedback. He is an ally who wants to nurture your growth, is invested in your future, and is thrilled when you succeed.

Furthermore, you aren't the only one who's trying to get a promotion at least every two years. If you have a high-achieving boss, expect that he will be receiving promotions quickly, too. That leaves a wake of rising vacant jobs available that you can grow into. Your boss knows your worth and can recommend you, giving you the chance to follow him up the corporate chain.

Finally, look for signs that your boss is considering you for an expected upward job vacancy. You might start getting invited to higher-level meetings or receiving more challenging projects. Don't get frustrated if he begins giving you more complex assignments that test your skills—it's probably a good sign.

A great boss will recognize your dedication and talent—and test you with stretch assignments to find out if you're ready for more responsibility. Rise to the challenge and dig into new projects with vigor. You'll expand your skillset, grow professionally, and maybe get a promotion sooner than you think.

> **Pro tip**: A great boss won't give you assignments or projects they don't think you can handle. He will make sure you have the tools and resources to do it well, but don't be afraid to ask for what you need. Remember, he's on your side.

EXAMINE EXTERNAL TIMING FACTORS

Every company is different, and there are always reasons that change the landscape for promotion opportunities over time. Some external factors are short-term, and some will last the entire time you work there. When it comes to getting your timing right, here are some external factors to be aware of while planning your career progression.

Recognize a change in regime

If there are changes in the C-suite—the highest level of the organization – you should prepare for a shift in company culture. You may want to ride out that wave of transformation and let the tides settle before you make a big ask for a promotion.

If your direct supervisor is on his way out and you have a great relationship, it can feel daunting to start over with a new boss, especially if you are well into your promotion campaign. Try to catch him before he leaves the company and ask if he will request your promotion. If he's parting ways on good terms, it's possible it will be accepted. At a minimum, ask him to put in a good word with your new manager.

Pro tip: Remember, if you don't ask, the answer is always no! Putting all that hard work into your promotion campaign is worthless if you never make the ask.

If your boss was suddenly fired for misconduct or let go for underperformance, it's best to focus on making a solid first impression and getting off on the right foot with your new supervisor. Don't immediately launch into promotion-mode with someone you hardly know.

Spend at least 30 days establishing a good working relationship and building mutual rapport. Demonstrate your talent and skills to build confidence and trust. Fill him in on what you were working on through regular check-ins. You don't have to start over completely, but you should take a step back to build a positive foundation with your new manager.

Is there a need?

If the company you work for is small, there might not be a good reason to promote anyone. Imagine the current team performs well and is a perfect match for the needs of the organization. Why would your boss choose to promote you—or anyone else?

Your boss won't develop an unnecessary position for you no matter how much they like you or how excellent you are at your job. Try to see it from his point of view. If you were in charge, would you conjure up a new role for someone just because they wanted a promotion? It's not a good business practice—not to mention it wouldn't be fair to the rest of the team.

If you don't see promotion opportunities on the horizon at your current company, assess your situation and decide what's most important to you. If you love the organizational culture, focus on demonstrating outstanding performance and give it a little time to see what develops over the next six months or so. On the other hand, if you're stagnant or bored, you won't be giving 100% at work, and that's not fair to anyone—including yourself. Explore moving to a new department or updating your resume to pursue the room to grow at another company.

Assess the financial health of the company

The financial well-being of every organization has an enormous impact on how long it will take to get promoted. If the company isn't profitable or is experiencing a hiring freeze, it may not be the best time to push hard for that promotion.

That's not to say it's impossible to get a promotion during an organizational financial hardship—there will still be some movement in personnel. For example, it might not be the best time to advocate for a new role designed specifically for you, but if there's a vacant position available that would be a step up, go for it! Just be aware that fiscal challenges will likely affect staff in every layer of the organization.

Acknowledge the effect of layoffs

If you notice an influx of layoffs in your department or across the company, it can be happening for several reasons—and it unquestionably means you can expect upcoming changes. In some cases, layoffs create possibilities for advancement—but proceed with caution.

For example, assume your department has nine people, and four of them are laid off over a month, including a supervisor. The company isn't going to replace the employees who were in a position parallel to yours, but a different type of manager is required.

You have a chance to apply for the supervisory position, but you'd be leading a much smaller team tasked with the same amount of work as before the layoffs. Carefully consider whether you're up to taking on long hours and increased responsibilities. It could be your chance to shine by leading a lean team and improving processes, but it will require a tremendous commitment. It's not for the faint of heart—make sure you're up for the challenge.

KEY TAKEAWAYS

- A lack of advancement can be a red flag to future employers. If you're not getting a promotion at least every two years, it's time to examine why.
- Don't ask to be promoted at your annual performance review. Focus on setting the stage for promotion with a long-term game plan, including regular check-ins.
- To get promoted fast, work in a high-growth industry or with a company that has clients in a growing field—and choose a great boss who is an advocate for your career progression.
- Be aware of external timing factors affecting your promotion, such as the need for new positions, layoffs, hiring freezes, changing leadership, and financial challenges.

CHAPTER 9.

BE PREPARED TO
MAKE THE ASK

You've done all the right things. You're great at your current job, you have periodic check-ins with your boss, you've enlisted an excellent mentor, and you've made allies with the highest performers in the office. Still, requesting a promotion can feel stressful or nerve-wracking—but it doesn't have to be. Equipping yourself with the right resources and knowledge will give you the confidence to start the conversation calm and collected.

INFORMATION YOU SHOULD HAVE READY

You learned to record your achievements in previous chapters, and you'll be glad you did when you ask for a promotion. It's a hassle to try to remember every victory you've accomplished at work. Even if you try, you'll likely forget some successes that will help your case. Furthermore, none of your accomplishments should be news to your boss since you've already discussed them during your regular check-ins. Here are some examples of things you should be documenting.

Examine your professional victories

As you review your accomplishments, keep your end goal in the forefront. What type of promotion are you seeking? Do you want to be a manager, or do you want to take on more complex assignments and projects? Tailor your successes to position yourself as a prime candidate for the job you want.

Don't worry about bringing every minor praise or victory to the meeting when you ask for your promotion. It will be overwhelming for your boss, and the overall message you're trying to convey may get lost in the shuffle. Instead, highlight the successes that show you'll excel at the job you want.

For example, imagine you're a novice customer service representative who has been with the company for almost two years. You're gearing up for a promotion to team manager. Make sure to document achievements such as doubling your customer satisfaction rate, or creating a new client retention strategy.

Furthermore, becoming a team leader will require more than service acumen—you'll have to be a proven leader. Plan ahead to demonstrate you have managerial skills among your peers—but tread lightly. You don't want to come across as bossy with your coworkers.

Help your colleagues succeed by offering advice when they ask for it. You could also start a monthly meeting where your team comes together to discuss challenges and best practices. It shows that you're committed to not only your own success—you're invested in the success of your team and the organization as a whole.

Gather positive feedback

You have to pitch yourself when you ask for a promotion, but the great things other people say about you can help immensely. Asking for a promotion is not the time to be overly humble. It's okay to brag on yourself a bit and show off the amount of praise you're getting.

Keep emails from customers who thank you for your help. Perhaps one of your vendors sent a note of appreciation that the marketing department used as a testimonial on the company website. Maybe a supervisor in a neighboring department left a note on your desk thanking you for volunteering for a project and working overtime.

For example, say you're a marketing specialist and a sales manager comes to your team to request help with an email campaign to attract leads for a new demographic. You step up to the plate and spearhead the campaign, even though you already have a full workload. The sales manager sends you an email saying, "Thank you so much for developing a seamless, high-impact email campaign. Our team appreciates your dedication and drive." Print that email and tuck it away in your "promotion folder," or save a copy in a folder on your computer.

If you pay attention, you'll likely see recognition of your exceptional work everywhere. Don't let it go to waste! Keep a running portfolio of praise for your efforts and highlight the best pieces—the ones that reflect your capacity for the job you desire. They'll certainly come in handy when you make the big ask.

Don't forget to be appreciative of your colleagues, vendors, and stakeholders. Remember to send them thoughtful emails and thank you letters. You'll feel great about making someone's day—and they'll return the favor more often than not.

> **Pro tip**: Are you familiar with the concept of "social proof"? Here it means that receiving praise from others will influence your boss—convincing him you are worthy of high praise. Think of it as earning a five-star rating via peer reviews on Amazon!

Recognize your market value

If you don't know how much your skills and talent are worth, how can you make a proper ask? Assess your value according to your experience, education, and skillset. In today's digital age, everything is online—it's not difficult to discern what you're worth when asking for a promotion.

However, evaluate the validity of your sources. In 2019, websites such as Glassdoor, Salary.com, and ZipRecruiter are familiar, trustworthy sites that share compensation packages, company reviews, benefits, and more. You may find that professionals with similar experience and training are making more money than you are—or have a more desirable title.

Use the information you find to build your case for promotion. Knowledge is power, and if you prove you have the data to back up your claim, you're more likely to get what you want.

> **Pro tip**: Turnover is expensive—companies want to retain the talent they value. If you can demonstrate that you're underpaid or merit a higher title, smart organizations will take action to keep you from leaving.

Assess whether you're ready to leave—or not

No matter how prepared you are, you might not get what you want in the end. If you love your job, the people you work with, and the mission of the organization, you may have to compromise. If that's the case, and your request for a promotion is denied, be ready to stick it out and keep working toward the next step. After all, if you talk about what other companies are offering but you're not willing to call it quits, your boss could counter with, "Well, why don't you go there?"

On the other hand, if you feel like you aren't getting anywhere and don't feel supported, you have nothing to lose. Give your boss the facts about what leading businesses in your industry offer top talent. Ask him what he'd be willing to do to keep you on his team. If you don't feel like your value is appreciated, it might be time to move on and start looking for a new job.

HOW TO PRESENT YOUR ASK

How you present your promotion matters just as much as the content of your ask. If you've been frustrated by a lack of advancement, it might be tempting to rant or complain. Avoid this at all costs!

Develop a presentation

Don't go overboard. You don't need to create a full-blown PowerPoint presentation that would rival a sales executives pitch to win a multi-million dollar account. It would come off as self-important, or even worse, a waste of valuable company time.

However, you should have your key talking points ready. You want to generate a meaningful conversation about your career and advancement in the company. You can print out documents, highlight the key points you will talk about, and make copies to share with your boss that you can look at together. Alternatively, you can create a PDF and project it on a larger computer monitor as you walk through them—consider which your manager would prefer.

No matter how you organize your information, it should contain everything this chapter has covered. Include the key metrics that support your success; praise from coworkers, clients, and stakeholders; industry compensation details; and any internal company data that paint a story about your value and highlight exemplary performance.

For example, if you're a sales representative, take advantage of the information at your disposal in your customer relationship management program (such as Salesforce). Capture month-over-month data that expose how you've steadily increased revenue and nurtured new accounts. Your boss might know you're generally doing well, but he won't necessarily take the time to mine that data and understand your value—so make it easy for him.

Finally, keep the conversation short. With proper preparation, the presentation shouldn't take more than 10 to 15 minutes. Plus, you want to leave time to answer questions, negotiate, and develop a plan with your boss.

Now that you know how to prepare for the ask, you'll discover precisely how to deliver it in the next chapter.

KEY TAKEAWAYS

- Never underestimate the importance of documenting your successes. Make it easy on yourself by keeping a running folder of victories—large and small—over time.
- Collect praise and positive feedback from colleagues, clients, vendors, and stakeholders. They are a critical part of your case for a promotion!
- Equip yourself with knowledge about your professional worth. Research and document salaries of workers with similar experience and education.
- Organize your thoughts and create a meaningful presentation about your desired promotion. Don't go overboard with an hour-long performance. Keep it short—10 to 15 minutes is all that's needed.

CHAPTER 10.

MAKING THE ASK

You've made all the right moves, and you're ready to ask for the promotion you want. It's normal to be a little nervous or experience a tinge of "stage fright," but you're prepared, confident, and ready. In this chapter, you'll learn precisely how to conduct an excellent ask.

THE NECESSITY OF THE ASK

Far too often, people put their heads down, work hard, and assume their supervisor will eventually notice them and *offer* a promotion. Sure, it could happen—but you could also get passed over for someone who took control of their career and asked for it themselves while you waited.

Don't expect your boss will notice you

Imagine you're doing your best work, getting excellent feedback from clients, vendors, and colleagues—and making your boss' life easier by being proactive and easy to manage. He still may not notice—remember, he's busy advancing his own career, too!

Even if your manager acknowledges your talent and work ethic—and thinks you're worthy of a promotion, it's unlikely he will promote you and give you a higher salary if you don't ask. Your boss has a budget to manage, and he's probably not going to allocate extra money toward your salary on his own.

To illustrate, imagine you visit a department store and find a coat marked down to $100, but you know it's worth at least $120. Would you offer to pay an extra $20 during checkout because you know the coat's real value? Of course not. You wouldn't offer to pay any more than what the price tag said. Apply the analogy to your career. Don't be the "great deal"—ask for the new title and the increased salary you deserve.

WHO TO ASK

Especially if you're early in your career, you might wonder, "Who's the appropriate person to ask for a promotion?" Do you go to human resources? Should you talk with your boss' supervisor?

Your boss is the gatekeeper

As you discovered in previous chapters, you should have initiated regular check-ins with your boss and be reviewing your progress toward mutually-agreed-upon goals over time. Your supervisor will have the information needed to advocate for your promotion—and a good boss will gladly do so when you've proven your value and clearly voice that you want to move up.

Don't go to human resources to ask about getting promoted. The first question they will ask is, "Have you talked with your supervisor about this?" Furthermore, it might get back to your boss that you went to HR—leaving him wondering why you didn't come to him first.

However, you can go to HR and inquire about *how* to ask for a promotion—it can be especially helpful if it's your first time asking for one. The human resources team is there to help recruit the best talent and further each employee's career with the company. They're likely to offer some great tips and suggestions for how to effectively approach your promotion request.

You also don't want to cross a boundary and approach your boss' manager about getting promoted. Imagine your boss meets with his supervisor, Jeff. Jeff says to your boss, "Oh, I meant to mention this to you. One of your team members, Jess, emailed me yesterday afternoon about promotion opportunities." Your boss has no idea, and quickly counters, "Okay—I'll carve out some time to talk with her about that."

Going around your boss will only undermine him, make him look like he doesn't know how to manage and communicate with his team, embarrass him, and potentially ruin the hard work you've done up to this point. The bottom line is that your boss is the gatekeeper, even if he doesn't make the final decision—he's the person with the power to move your request to the next stage.

Pro tip: If you aren't getting anywhere with your boss and he frequently cancels your check-ins, don't feel stuck. This situation is an excellent example of when it's a good

---

idea to visit with human resources and explore how to remove barriers to your advancement.

KNOW WHAT TO ASK FOR

A conversation about your promotion is different from the discussion you had with your hiring manager or human resources representative when you were offered an initial position. Here are some essential specifics you should consider.

Perfect your approach

It's entirely appropriate to negotiate your salary during an initial job offer. However, you shouldn't lead with asking for a certain amount of money when requesting a promotion. Instead of saying, "While I currently make $60,000 a year, I want to earn at least $75,000," try, "I believe I've proven I'm ready to move up and I'd like to be considered for a promotion."

Most larger, established companies have a structure or hierarchy in place, so when you ask for a promotion, you can generally expect what will happen when it's granted. Most organizations have established tiers of position titles and pay ranges—aim for a promotion to the next tier above your current position. For example, if you're a junior account manager, you should expect to be promoted to an account manager rather than a senior account manager.

Like anything else, there are exceptions to this rule of thumb. If you work in a smaller organization and you're demonstrating performance far above your job description, you might advance two levels. Alternatively, perhaps you accepted a position below your pay grade and skill level because you loved the potential, reputation, and culture of the company, but there wasn't an opportunity that matched your talent and experience. In this case, if someone two levels your senior leaves and you're a good fit for their position, you could move up faster.

Ask your boss to assess your situation

If an actual promotion isn't within your reach, you can politely ask your manager to assess your current situation and give you a proper raise. Make it clear that you're not requesting a standard cost-of-living increase.

Be your own advocate and ask for a merit raise—one based on your talent, accomplishments, and value as an employee. This strategy is particularly useful if you can prove you're paid less than your peers with similar titles and experience, or if you haven't received a raise in over a year. Simply ask if he can help catch you up to the rest of the industry with a boost in salary. If you're performing well, he's probably going to do what he can to keep you on board.

HOW TO ASK FOR THE PROMOTION

You know who to ask for a promotion (your boss), and what type of language to use. But what's the best delivery method for your big ask?

Always make the ask in person

It's critical to always ask for a promotion in a face-to-face meeting. Even if you and your boss work in separate locations, try to wait until he's in town for a visit. If that's not possible, schedule a video call at a minimum. Never make the ask in an email or physical letter.

Why is making the ask in person so significant? Nuances in body language, voice tone, and eye contact are a massive part of how people communicate. You want to send and receive them live. For example, if your boss winces, or crosses his arms and leans away—you'll know it's not a good sign and can tailor the rest of the meeting. If he smiles and nods, you can assume you're on the right track.

Furthermore, if you request the promotion in writing or through email, you may unintentionally come off as demanding, annoying, or unconfident. You don't have any control over what kind of mood your boss is in when he opens the email—you can't see his reactions, and he may even forward it to someone else. It should be a conversation between you and your boss only.

It may seem more daunting, but asking in person is always the best choice. A personal meeting adds psychological weight and importance to the matter. If you don't view it as important enough for an in-person discussion, then you aren't taking it quite seriously—and neither will your boss.

You've worked hard to get to this point, so take the time and effort to communicate with your boss properly. After all, communication skills are a vital part of demonstrating your capacity for leadership, so show your boss that you're confident and know how to handle delicate conversations with ease.

However, making the ask in person doesn't mean you can't document a paper trail. After the discussion, follow up with an email thanking your boss for his time. Include a summary of what you talked about and next steps. This way, if you aren't getting anywhere, or your boss leaves, you'll have proof that you took the initiative.

KEY TAKEAWAYS

- If you don't ask, the answer will always be no. You're unlikely to get promoted or receive a raise if you assume you'll eventually be noticed.
- Your boss is always the right person to talk to about your promotion. Don't sidestep him by going to his supervisor.
- You can visit with your human resources department for advice about the best way to ask for a promotion.
- Don't request a raise when you ask your boss for a promotion. Focus on the promotion first and let the dialogue evolve organically.
- Always request a promotion in person rather than through email or letters. You can document your ask in a follow-up email, if desired.

CHAPTER 11.

WHAT HAPPENS AFTER YOU ASK FOR A PROMOTION?

If you've followed the steps in the previous chapters, you've laid a strong foundation for finally earning a promotion. In this chapter, you'll learn how to handle the outcome of your ask—no matter the results.

PREPARING FOR THE OUTCOME

So now that you've requested a promotion, what happens next? You got the timing right, you made the ask specific and precise, and you had the metrics and recommendations to prove your value. However, it's unlikely that you'll get a response right away.

Asking for the status on your promotion

Waiting to hear back from your boss after you ask for a promotion can feel like waiting to find out how you scored on an important test in school. You don't want to come across as bothering or nagging your boss about the status of your promotion request. Lay the groundwork and prepare in advance. When you ask for the promotion, wrap up the conversation with something like, "Thanks for meeting with me and hearing me out. Is it okay for me to follow up with you on the status in two weeks?"

If two weeks go by and you haven't heard anything yet, email your supervisor and ask to schedule a quick meeting to review your request. Remember, just because your boss hasn't gotten back to you, it doesn't mean you should assume he has bad news.

The executives higher up in the company are often incredibly busy. Your boss may have to talk with other C-level team members about your request, and they may want to discuss the best way to shape your new role. Your boss will likely be glad you reminded him, provided that you agreed on two weeks and they have passed. It takes one more thing off his list to remember—and continues to showcase your initiative and drive.

However, read the terrain carefully. Some managers won't have the guts to tell you if the answer is no or if you aren't the right fit. If your boss seems to be dodging you in the office or when you ask for a status update—if he repeatedly says, "Oh yeah, Tim. I haven't forgotten. I'll get with Laura about that soon"—consider another avenue.

If you're not getting the answers you need from your boss, you can always go to human resources and ask what you should do next. It shows more diligence than storming into your boss' office with frustration and firing off heated questions about why he hasn't answered you yet. If you have a trusted mentor, you can also visit him or her for sage advice on actions you can take next.

WHEN YOU DON'T GET THE PROMOTION

No matter what the reason is, you're going to feel let down if you don't get the promotion after working so hard for it. However, your reaction speaks volumes about your future potential for advancement and how you handle challenges. If things don't go your way, keep your emotions in check— it will pay off in the future.

Run through your checklist

If you think you did everything right, but your request was denied, run through your actions at work over time. You should also examine whether there were any external factors that affected the decision.

Double check your market research to determine if you were actually being underpaid or had a lower title than others with your same level of experience and education. Don't forget to consider geographic circumstances. The cost of living, which varies by region, can affect salary ranges. For example, if you live in a rural part of the United States, you'll likely experience a lower cost of living compared to big cities such as Los Angeles or New York.

Review your last several performance appraisals. Did you consistently receive excellent reviews? If there were areas your boss wanted you to improve, does your work show that you did? It's also helpful to honestly assess your attitude. Did you exhibit too much frustration or neediness? Did you have frequent conflicts with coworkers?

HOW TO GET PROMOTED

Finally, evaluate whether your lack of promotion was due to personality or culture fit. Maybe the company has a reputation for not rewarding or recognizing top talent. Perhaps tenure is valued above all else. If you've run through your checklist and determined you and the company aren't a good fit, it's time to brush up your resume and think about moving on.

When someone else gets the promotion over you

When someone gets promoted over you, it's going to hurt—especially if you think (or know) they aren't the right person for the job. Life isn't fair, and the best candidate doesn't always win the promotion.

The hard truth is that the best person for the job doesn't always get it. It could be that your coworker made a more compelling case for promotion—maybe she sold her skillset or value more convincingly, even if she made promises she knows might be hard to keep. Perhaps the person who got promoted was guaranteed a promotion after one year in his particular position as a condition of accepting the job offer. Or maybe office politics favor specific employees – although this certainly isn't a positive company culture trait.

You might feel angry and tempted to start browsing for new jobs and sending out your resume to recruiters right away. But take a moment to gather yourself and your feelings. Don't start ugly office gossip about your newly promoted coworker or your boss—the last thing you want to do now is lose credibility and earn a reputation as a complainer. Don't make passive aggressive comments to anyone, either.

Pro tip: There's one caveat worth mentioning: if the person who's getting promoted over you is someone you've trained and helped develop over time, you should speak up. Unless there's something notably wrong with your performance, you should be moving up before one of your subordinates or someone who is clearly several steps behind you. Bring it up to your boss—it could be a managerial oversight that can be easily remedied. Just be sure to not put down the person who was just promoted.

When your boss gets promoted

What happens when you ask for a promotion, you don't get it…and you find out your boss got promoted? You've been proving yourself to your supervisor, taking projects off his plate, and showing that you have what it takes to advance. You probably feel like he's getting all the credit for your hard work.

If your boss is truly stealing the credit for work you've done, it's terrible for your career and suppresses your growth. It may be time to consider finding another department or looking for a job outside of the organization. Fortunately, this is a rare situation that doesn't happen very often. Most bosses aren't going to try to steal your thunder and leave you behind—they're going to appreciate your worth ethic and support your career development.

For instance, imagine your boss is advancing and has an excellent performance record—this is generally a good sign and can benefit you as well. As you've learned in previous chapters, a great boss who moves up will likely try to take you with him.

Furthermore, his promotion may leave a vacancy that creates an opportunity for you to move up. Even better, if you've done exceptional work for your boss and have a good working relationship, your career will likely benefit when he gains more influence with top executives in the company.

When you don't get the promotion you were promised

Imagine your current boss says he'll help you get a promotion but doesn't follow through. Or, say you were promised a promotion from a prior boss who is no longer with the organization or moved to another department.

No one can blame you for thinking the company should honor those promises. However, they're just meaningless commitments with no backbone. At best, all you can do is compile emails, chat messages, and any other communication proving your boss' intentions and bring that documentation to human resources.

For example, your old boss may have submitted paperwork to approve your promotion and it either hasn't been processed yet or got lost in the shuffle after he was already out the door.

Most likely, however, your previous supervisor wanted to avoid a tough conversation and neglected to address it before leaving. Plus, your new boss will want to assess and evaluate your performance before immediately promoting you.

WHEN YOU GET THE PROMOTION

When you're finally promoted after all of your hard work, you're going to feel elated and relieved. Let's conclude by learning how to accept your promotion gracefully.

When you get promoted over your peers

If you find yourself in a position where you get promoted over your peers, it can be awkward—especially if you become the boss of your former peers. Perhaps you typically go to lunch together or even have friendships outside of the office with coworkers you beat out for a promotion.

You might feel tempted to hide or downplay your promotion, particularly if you want to be sensitive to others' feelings or don't like the limelight. However, don't conceal your success by asking human resources not to announce your promotion or not updating your email signature to reflect your new title.

If your peers and friends at work are genuine, they'll be happy for you. Even if they are a little jealous, they will be proud and cheer you on! Celebrate your promotion with a spirit of humility and continue to support your colleagues the same way they do for you.

Remember, you earned it!

Thank your boss for his support, but keep in mind that you earned this promotion on your own accord. No one did you any favors—this is your payoff! You followed the steps and set the stage for your own success.

For some high performers or those who work in companies with frequent promotions, an advancement is simply an expected step up the corporate ladder. It's a great sign that your excellent work is being recognized—and that you're working for an organization worthy of your talent.

Either way, getting a promotion is great for your self-esteem and boosts your motivation levels and happiness at work. The salary increases that come with promotions also transform the way you think about things like debt, savings, vacations, and your overall financial goals. Money certainly isn't everything—but being rewarded for your hard work is great!

Don't forget, promotions come with added responsibilities and an adjustment period that can be a bit stressful. Expect new duties and give yourself time to acclimate to your new role—you've proven you can handle it!

KEY TAKEAWAYS

- Whether you get the promotion or not, focus on making it a positive learning experience and practicing continual self-improvement.
- If your request is denied, take the time to analyze your checklist, your performance, attitude, and the company culture.
- If someone gets promoted over you, keep your emotions in check. Remember, the best candidate doesn't always get the job.
- If your boss promised you a promotion and left, bring evidence of your communications to human

resources. Be patient and keep working hard with your new boss.

- If your boss gets promoted over you, it's not necessarily a bad thing—it might open up new opportunities for you! If they stole your credit, consider moving on.
- When you do receive a promotion, accept it gracefully and remember that you earned it.

CHAPTER 12.

NEXT STEPS

That's it! You should now feel ready to launch your campaign for your next promotion.

I'd love to hear your success stories, or help with your stumbles or struggles until you get there. Please share by emailing me at promoted@anthonyspark.com.

IF YOU LIKED THIS BOOK...

Thanks for reading. If you enjoyed this book, and have a moment to spare, I'd really appreciate a short review. Please consider leaving an honest review on Amazon, GoodReads, BookBub, or your favorite store.

Join my email list for a chance for a free copy of my next book, as well as other giveaways and pre-release specials at: https://anthonyspark.com/join

ABOUT THE AUTHOR

Anthony S. Park is host of the popular podcast *Simple Money Wins* (available on <u>YouTube</u>, <u>iTunes</u>, and <u>anthonyspark.com</u>).

He is a New York executor, attorney, and entrepreneur. Anthony's cases have been featured in many places, including the *Wall Street Journal*, *New York Times*, CNBC, and *MarketWatch*.

ALSO BY ANTHONY S. PARK

How to Buy Your Perfect First Home: What Every First-Time Homebuyer Needs to Know

How Probate Works: A Guide for Executors, Heirs, and Families

How to Hire an Executor: For Your Loved One's Estate or Your Will

INDEX

A
achievers, association with, 46
Always be Learning (ABL) mindset, 33–34
annual performance review, 60–61
annual raises, 13–14
appreciation for colleagues/vendors/stakeholders, 72
assessment by boss, 81
A-team, association with, 45–46
attention by decision-makers, 43–59
attitude in office, 28–29
attitude of employee, 22
autonomy, increased responsibilities and, 31–32

B
bonuses, 9
boss, assessment by, 81
boss, exceptional, 63–64
boss, high-achieving, 63–64
boss, promotion of, 89
boss, reviewing progress, 78
boss-employee relationships, 22

C
catch-up raises, 14–16
check-in meetings, frequency of, 55
check-in scheduling, 33, 54
checklist, running through, 87–88
colleagues, involving in workflow, 36
comfort zone, 45
commitment to organizational culture, 26
communications, from recruiters, 31

promotion opportunities, 66–67
promotion request, right approach for, 80–81
promotions, defined, 5
promotion-worthy performance, 52
publications in line of work, 47

Q
quick promotion, 62–68

R
raise, based on performance, 16
raise without promotion, 13–18
readiness to move up, 33–41
recruiters, 6, 31
red flags in professional background, 59–60
refusal of promotion, 87–90
reputation, building, 28
reputation as control freak, 36
reputation building, 28
request for promotion, 56
request for promotion, aftereffects, 85–93
request for promotion, in person, 82
request for promotion, necessity of, 77–83
request for promotion, preparation, 69–75
responsibilities, increased and autonomy, 31–32
responsibilities with promotion, 7–9
resume, 20–22, 21
revenue generation, 45
right time for promotion, 60–61
routine check-ins, 51–52
Rule of Seven, for sales/marketing, 55–56

Made in the USA
San Bernardino, CA
09 March 2020